THE
FOUR LEVELS
TOWARDS HAPPIEST

THE FOUR LEVELS TOWARDS HAPPIEST

Father David Scotchie

Uramado Press

The Four Levels Towards Happiest

Copyright 2025 by Father David Scotchie.
All rights reserved.

No part of this book may be used or reproduced in any manner whatsoever without permission except in the case of brief quotations embodied in critical articles or reviews.

Contact frdavidscotchie@gmail.com

Book and Cover Layout: Tim Schoenbachler

Facebook: www.facebook.com/frdavidscotchie

Scripture texts in this work are taken from the New American Bible, revised edition © 2010, 1991, 1986, 1970 Confraternity of Christian Doctrine, Washington, D.C. and are used by permission of the copyright owner. All Rights Reserved. No part of the New American Bible may be reproduced in any form without permission in writing from the copyright owner.

DEDICATION

To the eternal happiness of my
nieces and nephews and their spouses and children

Table of Contents

Introduction 9

What Makes Us Happier?
        LEVEL ONE – Feeling Good 13

What Makes Us Happier?
        LEVEL TWO – Having the Goods 35

What Makes Us Happier?
        LEVEL THREE – Doing Good 51

What Makes Us Happiest?
        LEVEL FOUR – God Is Good 71

Why Wait? 93

Endnotes 97

Introduction

"Can I ask you a quick question for a documentary I'm doing?" The camera phone focused on a 72-year old woman in hiking shorts at Arches National Park.

"Sure," the woman smiled at the camera.

The off-screen voice said, "The question is, 'Are you happy?'"

After the 2020 COVID pandemic, Atdhe Trepca quit his filmmaking job and traveled the country with his camera and his quick question.[1] He approached a 20-something stranger at the gas station, a young couple on the sidewalk, and a double amputee man in an electric scooter. "Can I ask a quick question? Are you happy?"

"No," the man with no legs shook his head. "Who is?" He answered his own question. "Unless you're rich or live on your own island. No."

A woman in a park replied, "The definition of my happiness is not family. It's not friends. It's more a state of mind." She got more specific. "Happiness is you get up in the morning and the first thing you say is wow, I woke up." The woman smiled big. "My happy is making other people happy."

Trepca posted the videos on TikTok and now has almost four million followers.[2]

Are you happy? Is your boyfriend or girlfriend happy? Your husband or wife wants to be happy. Your children want to be happy. Your co-workers want to be happy. I certainly want to be happy. Do you know anyone who does not want to be happy? We are wired for happiness. The pursuit of happiness is so self-evident that it is listed as an inalienable right in the United States Declaration of Independence.

I would like to suggest that a better question than "Are you happy?" or "What makes you happy?" is "What makes you happier?" We know from our own experience that happiness is not an all-or-nothing experience. At times we are more happy. At times we are less happy. Exploring the idea that we can be happy, happier, and happiest, the four sections of this booklet examine four ways we can pursue happiness. Each pursuit of happiness has some good, some bad, and some ugly consequences.

I would like to thank my careful readers: JoAnn Elder, Dianne Kramer, Father Augustine Clark, and Brandon Shintani. I owe a debt of gratitude to Father Bill Bruning. He told me about a talk he had heard on the four levels of happiness. His description of the talk inspired me to give a homily based on it. After people told me that they got a lot out of the homily, I wrote this booklet. I wrote it especially for those who were not likely to have heard my Sunday Mass homily. I wrote is as a Catholic priest

INTRODUCTION

and the pastor of Nativity Catholic Church in Longwood, Florida. I want it to help you become truly happier.

This booklet is not meant to be read cover-to-cover like a novel. Each section concludes with three reflection questions and three action steps. Happiness does not just happen. We have to do our part.

You who are spiritual but not religious can skip the memory verse from scripture that follows the reflection questions. The *Catechism of the Catholic Church* references will likely not do much for you. Of course, the more background you have in the Bible and the Catholic faith, the more these things will mean to you. Even if you know nothing about the saints, I encourage you to find out more. Their stories inspire us!

A warning: The fourth and happiest level will not make you happy. At least not at first.

What Makes Us Happier?
LEVEL ONE
Feeling Good

Feeling Good: The Good

What makes us happy? There is truth to the saying, "Eat, drink, and be merry!" We feel good when we eat a fat hamburger with a supersize side of French fries and a cold milkshake. Our taste buds, hardwired by the survival of the fittest, tuck away sweets and fats. We like to relax with an adult drink at the end of a hard day at work. Have two drinks and we feel no pain.

Breaking a sweat in the gym two or three times a week relieves stress and produces endorphins. Exercise makes us feel stronger, more attractive, confident, and happier.

We feel good when we get attention. The clever people in Silicon Valley know this. They reward us with notifications, bubbles, likes, and video feeds on our cell phones. The dings get our attention by giving us attention which makes us feel good.

Music makes us feel good. Listening to the Oldies warms the heart with nostalgia. A Beethoven symphony stirs the soul while a Taylor Swift song can fit any mood. We feel good when we sing in the shower.

Dogs make us feel good. They jump and bark at the sight of us. Petting their soft fur is calming. They do not argue with us, make sarcastic remarks, or give us the silent treatment.

The Four Levels Towards Happiest

Children live in the Feeling Good zone for good reason. They thrive when they eat, drink, and get loving attention. They love lullabies and make up their own songs. The abstract world is not for them. Give them a cuddly Winnie-the-Pooh stuffed bear and they will carry it until its arms fall off. A child is not concerned with the pursuit of happiness. They simply do what makes them feel good. For them, this is good!

Feeling Good: The Bad

I have liked to write a daily gratitude list. Number one on my daily gratitude list was air conditioning. Since Florida weather most of the year was a free sauna, air conditioning usually topped my gratitude list. Next on the gratitude list? Chocolate! Dark chocolate, they said, was good for you. That was all the rationale I needed to put chocolate on my list. I added breakfast, lunch, and dinner. My car was on my list. It was reliable. It had air conditioning. Its radio tuned in a classical music HD station. I was grateful for my car. And so went my gratitude list. One day looking over my gratitude list, I noticed that it was a list of things that made me feel good. They were small pleasures. Although there was no harm in any of these pleasant things for which I was grateful, they were self-centered. My Inner Child thrived on the day's small pleasures even as my Adult Man stood on the sidelines.

The consequence of my pursuit of small pleasures came to the fore one Lent during daily Mass. I sat in my presider's chair imagining, "A hot cup of coffee would hit the spot." The lector read the first reading from the Scriptures. I never heard it. I was distracted by that anticipated cup of coffee. One cup would be good, I thought, but two cups would be too much. Without intending it, I was at Mass but not really present. Even as

I realized how coffee had a hold on my attention, I could not drop the thought and give the Mass my undivided attention. My mind was intent on enjoying a cup of coffee. The solution? Give up coffee for Lent. I simply took coffee off my menu for forty days. Once coffee was no longer on the menu, I could see what the cup of coffee was really about. I came to understand that daydreaming about a cup of coffee was not really about a cup of coffee. It was about feeling good for the moment instead of feeling bored with the familiar Mass. Removing the distraction of a cup of coffee freed me to pay attention to my boredom. What I needed was not a cup of coffee. What I really needed was to prepare for Mass with more prayer and intention.

The downside of the pursuit of happiness through feeling good is that our Inner Child gets fat and happy for the moment while our Adult Self shrivels. Our Inner Child can eat a pint of Rocky Road ice cream to fill up a lonely evening. We can forward cute cat videos rather than face a difficult decision. We can chase infatuation rather than make true friendships. The pursuit of feeling good leaves us empty. It sidetracks us from growing up.

One graduation season I attended two high school graduations. Except for the colors of the robes, the two graduations followed the same script. The color guard brought in the flags. We stood and said the Pledge of Allegiance, ending with the inspirational, "…one nation, under God, with liberty and justice for all." The chorus sang, and then the speeches began.

The speakers promised that the world was your oyster. "You can be whoever you want to be," the commencement speakers gushed, "when you make up your mind and do it." The valedictorian speech encouraged the graduates to persevere, like a boulder in a river, not going with the current but standing our ground. A salutatorian speech told us to learn from our failures. Above all, the speeches exhorted us, "Follow your passion! Chart your own course! March to the beat of your own drummer!"

The assumption behind these speeches was that when we follow our passion, we will be happy. That's how it works, right? Not quite. What was missing in those speeches was the mention of anyone else. Like a giant selfie, the speeches pictured us with our own dreams, our own hopes, our own desires, and our own hard work. There was no one else in the picture.

Our culture has taught us to tell our adulting children, "I don't care what work you do, just do whatever makes you happy." In other words, do whatever makes you feel good. In pursuit of feeling good, we restlessly pursue that white whale of happiness and jump from job to job and relationship to relationship, misled by feeling good.

The Bible paints a different picture. After the terrible events in Jerusalem where Jesus had been arrested by a mob, falsely accused in a kangaroo court, tortured, lynched, and buried in the tomb, the disciples returned home to Galilee. On the mountaintop, a favorite place for them to gather in prayer, the risen Jesus appeared to them. Resurrected from the dead but only moments before ascending to heaven, Jesus gave his final words to his disciples. Like a graduation speech, he sent his followers into the world with a final command. He said, "Go and make disciples." He did not say, "Go and fulfill yourself." He did not say, "Go and do what makes you feel good." He did not say, "Go and pursue happiness." He did not even raise the bar to "try to be kinder." Jesus simply said, "Go and make disciples." In other words, "It is not about you."

Jesus' command, "Go and make disciples," makes modern people feel uncomfortable. Who was he to tell people what to do? What about respect for personal freedom? No wonder religion turns people off. It makes them feel uncomfortable.

As a teenager, I stood on the sidelines watching the game of life, expecting that my passion would take my hand and lead me. Even though I had heard the words, "Be a priest," I had said "No." Being a priest was not my idea. I did not know what I wanted, only that I wanted what I wanted. Age appropriate for a tenth grader, what I really wanted was to be in charge. When I slowly let go of the illusion that I could figure out my life and go live it, I found joy and peace, passion and happiness. Rather than finding yourself, the purpose of life is to lose yourself. Our feeling good culture insists, "It is all about you." Here's the whole truth: Where your deepest passion meets the world's deepest need, there you find real happiness.

Another consideration in the pursuit of happiness is the reality of suffering. We get sick. We do not get what we want. People treat one another terribly. A way of life must deal with the fact that we suffer. When feeling good is supposed to be the way to happiness, how does suffering fit in? We act as a child would act. We avoid the things that make us feel bad. We double down on the things that make us feel good. Escape is how our Inner Child reacts to suffering. In the short term, avoidance and escape may work. In the long term, the refusal to face suffering leads to greater suffering – addictions. (More on that in the next section.)

A final consideration in the pursuit of happiness is ethics. The Prime Directive, also known officially as Starfleet General Order 1, is an ethical principle in the "Star Trek" TV shows and movies. It prohibits Starfleet crews from interfering with the natural social and technological development of alien civilizations. The Prime Directive's purpose is to protect less advanced cultures. Exposure to the socially advanced Starfleet and its advanced technology such as warp drive could cause unintended harm to other cultures.[3]

What is the Prime Directive when feeling good is the highest value? The imperative is to avoid making people uncomfortable. We are quick to affirm and slow to challenge. Rather than discussing and debating the truth of a matter, we are more concerned about triggering trauma. We let feelings decide whether or not something is "right." Someone saying, "What you are saying makes me uncomfortable," is a cue to shut down the conversation.

Feeling good censures our behavior. For example, we might have grown up saying a blessing before meals, but when dining with non-religious friends or in a restaurant we skip the usual blessing before eating because we do not want to make others uncomfortable. Elderly members of my parish tell me that they have decided not to have a funeral Mass, the most important "last rites" they can receive, because their children have not been at Mass in years and would be "uncomfortable" when everyone else is receiving Holy Communion and they are not. The grandchildren have not even been baptized. The fear of making family or friends uncomfortable replaces the greatest prayer we can offer for the dead with a feel-good "celebration of life." Such is the Prime Directive of feeling good. It gives our feelings veto power over choices that do not feel good.

Level One – Feeling Good

Feeling Good: The Ugly

Feeling Good turns ugly when it becomes the go-to way to deal with trauma and unwanted feelings. It takes on a life of its own. For example, loneliness is a lousy feeling that no one wants. We are made to love and be loved. The human heart desires genuine relationships. Yet loneliness has grown in our individualistic society. In 2014, Americans spent just under 40 hours each week alone. In 2021, Americans spent almost 48 hours each week alone, an increase of 20% in seven years. Nearly eight in ten Gen Zers and seven in ten Millennials are lonely, versus half of Boomers. Social media reinforced by the COVID-19 pandemic has marked a generation with isolation. Artificial Intelligence is getting so humanlike that it crowds out real connections and leads to AIsolation.[4]

Pornography offers an immediate feel-good solution. It gives momentary relief. The use of pornography to cure loneliness though is much, much worse than the loneliness. Exploiting brain chemistry and social media, pornography cripples the person's ability to give of the self in friendship and love. It distances the person from reality itself. The porn way to feel better when lonely rapidly becomes a compulsion that creates greater isolation, loneliness, and misery.[5] Looking for love and happiness, one can quickly end up trapped in a dark place.

The Four Levels Towards Happiest

Do you use pornography to feel better? Does a friend or family member use pornography? The following questions can help assess the situation. (Pornography is only one of the many ways we self-medicate. You can substitute in the following questions other feel-good activities: alcohol, smoking, vaping, prescription drugs, illegal drugs, social media, shopping, gaming, sports betting, eating, and so on.)[6]

- Do you feel empty or shameful after viewing porn and wish you could stop?
- Have you ever promised yourself that you would never again view porn?
- Have you lied to your family members, church leaders, or others about your porn use?
- Does your use of porn interfere with, limit, or reduce the social, occupational, educational, or recreational areas of your life?
- Have you stayed up late at night or woken up during the night to view porn?
- Do you erase history, "cover tracks," and take steps to hide your porn use to avoid being caught?
- Do you view more porn and for longer periods of time than you initially intend?
- Do you find yourself viewing different types of porn, perhaps outside your sexual orientation, to feel the desired excitement?

Level One – Feeling Good

- Do you minimize your porn viewing by using statements like "Everyone is doing it," "No one is getting hurt," or "This is not as bad as what others do"?

Immediate gratification makes us feel good – at first. When used for the wrong purpose, it destroys our happiness – forever.

Getting trapped in the ugly corruption of feeling good is far more than an individual moral failing. Much of the American economy conspires to make money from immediate gratification. Advertising used to call attention to the qualities of a product or service. Now it shows us appealing, laughing people. "It's one thing to buy well-made shoes because they protect your feet and look attractive. It's another to buy yet one more pair of shoes because advertisers have convinced you that your present life is shabby, but this next purchase will finally make you happy." The "attention economy" is an addiction economy. "Practically every aspect, down to the shade of red that alerts you to a new comment or like, has been calibrated not to make you wiser or happier but to get you hooked."[7]

The story of Naaman shows a way of hope.

Naaman (NAY-a-man) was the commander-in-chief of the kingdom of Aram. In biblical times, Aram was at times an ally of Israel and at times an enemy of Israel. Although he had position and power, Naaman suffered from some sort of humiliating and chronic skin ailment.

On the advice of an Israelite slave girl, Naaman traveled the long journey to the Israelite prophet Elisha (ee-LI-shuh) in Samaria to be healed. His horses and chariots were loaded with ten silver talents, six thousand gold pieces, and ten festal garments. Upon arriving, Elisha the prophet did not bother coming to the door! Rather, Elisha sent Naaman the message to wash seven times in the Jordan river.

What do you think Naaman did? Did he wash seven times in the Jordan river? NO! Naaman stomped off. "Who does this guy think he is? He did not even meet me in person. Doesn't he know who I am? Surely he should come out to me and stand there to call on the name of the LORD his God, and move his hand over the place, and thus cure the leprous spot." In any case, he added, were not the mighty mountain rivers of Damascus cleaner than the muddy Jordan creek?

I cannot read the story of Naaman without thinking of the good men and women addicted to lust. They pray their rosary until the beads fall apart. They vow not to look at certain websites or visit certain places. They lock their smartphones with special filters and passwords. All to no avail. Despite their best efforts, they sink deeper into shame and isolation, as sick as their secret. Like Naaman, they bring all their prestige and power and wealth and skill to the problem yet fall again and again.

Naaman's servant pleaded for him to reconsider. "My father, if the prophet told you to do something extraordinary, would you not do it? All the more since he told you, 'Wash, and be clean'?"

Something in the plea changed his heart. Naaman set aside his way and took the plunge. As Elisha the prophet had directed, he washed in the Jordan river seven times. Lo and behold, "His flesh became again like the flesh of a little child, and he was clean."[8]

Those of you with a spouse or son or father using porn, here is what you cannot do. You cannot nag or scold or shame or threaten. You cannot change him or her. Instead, what you must do is everything they should be doing to be freed from their addiction. You must pray hard and long on your knees, learn about addictions, get connected with people in your situation, talk to a therapist, and above all surrender yourself and the whole thing to God. It is not fair. You did not cause this grave problem, but there it is.

One thing you can do. Like Naaman's servant, you can suggest. "My father, if the prophet told you to do something extraordinary, would you not do it? All the more since he told you, 'Wash, and be clean'?"

Naaman was healed when he set aside his power and prestige and took the plunge. Twelve Step programs such as Alcoholics Anonymous are not self-help programs. Relying on the self is the problem! "The crucial change in attitude began when we admitted we were powerless, that our habit had us whipped".[9] Those who sponsor themselves quickly relapse.

Those who do what their sponsors tell them to do – go to meetings, make phone calls, and work the steps – experience recovery. Relying on the wisdom of others who had gone that way before, they come to make real connections and live in joyous freedom as God intended.

For men, this is especially hard. We expect we must do great things to achieve a great healing. What healed Naaman and countless others though was not great achievement but great humility. They did what they were told to do. They did the next right thing.

Father Joe (not his real name) was a good priest full of zeal for his parish. But he got into steroids and homosexual relationships. He got busted. His story made the newspapers and local TV news. His bishop pulled him from the parish and sent him to an in-patient treatment facility. After six months, he returned to his diocese. He worked in the chancery on a short leash. Then he worked in a parish under close supervision. He went to Twelve Step meetings, met regularly with his sponsor, and made phone calls daily. After years of hard work and grace, the bishop made him pastor of a parish. Since the internet is forever, the parishioners knew about his past. They loved him anyway. He came to sponsor others struggling with addictions. He was made dean of priests for his region. He was a happy man.

What healed Father Joe and countless others was not great achievement but great humility. Like Naaman, they took the plunge and did what they were told to do.

Level One – Feeling Good

Naaman offered Elisha the gold and silver in payment. Elisha refused. God's healing was a gift, free of charge! Naaman, with Elisha's permission, instead took two muleloads of Israelite dirt. He wanted to worship Elisha's Lord in his own land. So he took some land with him. Elisha bid him farewell. "Go in peace."

Reflection Questions

1. How do I rely on small pleasures – food, entertainment, scrolling, shopping, drinking – to avoid boredom, loneliness, or deeper questions about my life?
2. How has a habit that makes me feel good kept me from being mentally and emotionally present in important moments or relationships?
3. Where is life inviting me to humility – like Naaman – so that healing can begin beyond my own willpower?

Scripture Verse

"He has made everything beautiful in its time; He has also set eternity in the human heart." – *Ecclesiastes 3:11*

Action Steps

1. Create a Daily Gratitude List – But Look Deeper

At the end of each day this week, write down three things for which you are grateful. Make sure at least one of these is not a pleasure but something that shapes you: a person who supported you, a meaningful challenge you faced, or a moment of clarity. This practice helps shift gratitude from comfort to growth.

2. Fast From One Feel Good Habit for Seven Days

Choose one habit that gives you quick comfort – such as late-night snacking, social media scrolling, surfing the TV, or impulse online shopping – and set it aside for seven days. During that time, simply notice what emotions arise when the habit is no longer available. Pay attention to what the craving reveals about deeper needs, stress, or longings beneath the surface.

3. Begin or End the Day With Five Minutes of Stillness

Find a quiet place, silence your devices, and sit comfortably. Take slow breaths. Let your thoughts settle like sediment in still water. Gently acknowledge whatever comes to mind – desires, worries, frustrations, hopes – and ask for grounding, clarity, and peace as you enter or close the day.

Relevant Citations from the *Catechism of the Catholic Church*

1. **CCC 1718** – The human desire for happiness comes from a deeper place than momentary pleasure.
2. **CCC 1762–1766** – Emotions are good but must be integrated into a whole, healthy life.

3. **CCC 1809** – Temperance moderates pleasures so they contribute to well-being rather than control us.

St. Augustine of Hippo (4th–5th century)

Patron saint of: seekers, brewers, those with difficult pasts. Augustine spent years chasing pleasures, relationships, and achievements, only to discover that the restlessness inside him could not be soothed by comfort alone. His long journey toward honesty, humility, and purpose mirrors the shift from the pursuit of pleasure to deep, lasting fulfillment.

St. Thérèse of Lisieux (19th century)

Patron saint of: missionaries, florists, those seeking simplicity. Thérèse struggled with emotional sensitivity, insecurity, and longing for affirmation. Yet she discovered that joy grew not from comfort but from small daily acts of honesty, humility, and love. Her "Little Way" demonstrates how meaning emerges when we let go of the constant chase for pleasant feelings.

St. Mark Ji Tianxiang (d. 1900)

Patron saint of: those struggling with addiction. Mark Ji battled opium addiction for decades, continually seeking healing even when he felt unworthy. He remained sincere in his desire for freedom and ultimately gave his life as a martyr during the Boxer Rebellion. His story powerfully mirrors Naaman's: healing often begins when we surrender pride and acknowledge our need for help.

What Makes Us Happier?
LEVEL TWO
Having the Goods

Having the Goods: The Good

When I visit the hospital, I ask the patient lying in the hospital bed, "What do you want to pray for?" They look at me like I have two heads. "My health!" No hesitation. What else would anyone want to pray for? If you do not have your health, you do not have anything. I gamely follow up. "Besides your health, what else might you pray for?" They pause. After some consideration, they might add, "My family." "My grandkids." "Peace on earth." Rarely does a person say, "My immortal soul."

Make no mistake, health is good! Given the choice between good health and bad health, who would not want to be strong in leg and arm, able to leap tall buildings with a single bound. Good health allows us to travel rather than be tied to the bathroom. Good health gives us the freedom to do what we want to do.

We want to have a good name among our peers. We want to have a good job that gives security to our families and an income to support a certain lifestyle. We want to live in a good house in a good neighborhood with good schools. In short, we want to have the Good Life.

Unlike the immediate gratification of Feeling Good, we are willing to delay gratification to Have the Goods. We sacrifice now to have later. In our student years, we study hard and skimp on the fun and games. We take on debt to get a good education. In our work, we put in the extra hours. We spend time on the job rather than with family or sports in order to get a future position with higher pay. We rent while we save our money to buy a house. We drive a clunker while looking forward to having a brand new car. We work now and play later when we will be able to afford fancy restaurants, vacations abroad, and cruises to exotic ports.

Achievement of wealth, status, and power can bring a sense of satisfaction. They can provide for raising a family. Having the Goods brings us a measure of happiness.

LEVEL TWO – HAVING THE GOODS

Having the Goods: The Bad

Joe DiMaggio won nine World Series titles with the New York Yankees. Babe Ruth and Mickey Mantle won seven. Yankee captain Derek Jeter and ace reliever Mariano Rivera won five titles together. Yet after ten years of Hall of Fame play in the lineup of the most famous franchise paying a $300 million payroll for a roster full of stars, how many World Series titles did superstar slugger Aaron Judge hold? Zero. Following the Yankees' 2025 play-off defeat at the bats of the Toronto Blue Jays in a best-of-five division series, Aaron Judge said, "When you don't win, it's not a good year."[10]

The downside of Having the Goods is that we can never have enough. We are not satisfied with a winning record. We want to win the World Series. We always want more health, more wealth, more success, and more status. We climb to the top of the ladder only to discover it is leaning against the wrong wall. Satisfaction in this year's achievement eventually runs into frustration. When we fall short, it's not a good year.

When Having the Goods is the way to happiness, what is the meaning of suffering? Suffering becomes a sign of the lack of achievement. The spiritual writer Henri Nouwen described this view. "If we remain uneducated, poor, or unemployed, if we have an unhappy marriage or uncooperative children, the main reason is that we have simply not tried hard enough...We have been lazy, undisciplined, immoral, or just stupid."[11] The remedy is to try harder. We double down. When we still do not achieve what we want, we likely blame others – the boss, the spouse, immigrants, the government, the economy – while secretly feeling shame for our failure to achieve.

Because much of our American economy runs on Feeling Good, Having the Goods drives American society. "We are so dedicated to the goal of ever-increasing growth and development that we cannot imagine anyone being elected to public office without promising to increase the nation's wealth and power.... If anything is certain, it is that this nation desires to be the best, the strongest, and the most powerful. The attitude of 'We're number one!' is nurtured with all diligence and on all levels: in athletics, business, technology, and military power."[12] From this perspective, those who do not have the goods – prisoners, elderly, disabled – have no one to blame but themselves.

A used 203-foot superyacht was selling secondhand for only $90M in March 2022 at the Palm Beach International Boat Show. What doubled the pleasure of the wealthy was yacht envy. They paid a premium to dock their yachts near the restaurant of the yacht club so that all could see them. Such wealth leads to power. At the American presidential inauguration in January 2025, the three richest people in the world – Mark Zuckerberg of Facebook, Jeff Bezos of Amazon, and

Level Two – Having the Goods

Elon Musk of SpaceX and Tesla – stood on the stage with the new president. On his other side, Sergey Brin, the cofounder of Google, and Tim Cook, CEO of Apple, joined them. "There were so many billionaires onstage that the leaders of Congress were relegated to the audience."[13]

"We paradoxically see the growth of a wealthy elite, living in a bubble of comfort and luxury, almost in another world compared to ordinary people," Pope Leo XIV wrote. "The illusion of happiness derived from a comfortable life pushes many people towards a vision of life centered on the accumulation of wealth and social success at all costs, even at the expense of others and by taking advantage of unjust social ideals and political-economic systems that favor the strongest."[14] Our pursuit of happiness through achievement has consequences. Inequality in power leads to unjust systems. The misery of the many becomes buried by indifference and self-congratulation. The strong get stronger and many more suffer.

These ideas take on flesh in Kazuo Ishiguro's novel, *Klara and the Sun*. The story is set in a future in which affluent parents have their children "lifted," a genetic-enhancement process that makes their children smarter. The humanoid robot Klara was an AF, or Artificial Friend for a sickly girl Josie. Programmed to understand and mimic the complexity of human interactions, Klara noted that Josie's mother dressed in "high-rank office clothes" and deduced that clothes signaled status. On one occasion, the mother hosted a social for Josie's class. The classmates mocked Rick, Josie's neighbor and only true friend, because he was not successfully "lifted." Klara noted how the adults and their children strived for status yet remained unhappy. By the end of the novel, Klara herself, though only an AF, was the happiest because she sacrificed herself for others.

With Feeling Good, the prime directive was to avoid making someone uncomfortable. The implied limit to one's efforts to feel good was another's discomfort. With Having the Goods, the prime directive is captured by Google's one-time unofficial motto, "Do no evil." (Who determines what is evil and what is good remains unsettled.) "Do no evil" places an implied limit to Having the Goods. Your achievement cannot cause harm to another. In practice, conflicts abound. For example, pollution and environmental exploitation affect poor communities more than affluent ones. Rather than "do no evil," the unspoken ethical imperative for Having the Goods is a modified Golden Rule, "Those with the gold make the rules."

Having the Goods: The Ugly

When the four U.S. Navy ships with sixty-one cannon sailed into Tokyo Bay on July 8, 1853, Commodore Perry dramatically ended two hundred and fifty years of Japanese isolation and peace. The Japanese shogun was powerless to expel the American military. After the show of force, Perry sailed home. With the Civil War brewing, the Americans lost interest in the Pacific.

The Japanese, however, learned the lesson well. They saw how the western powers carved up Asia and Africa, subjugated non-Christian countries, enslaved their people, and exploited their natural resources. Japan remade its society to build a strong military. Japanese children sang a new song, "There is a Law of Nations it is true. But when the moment comes, remember the Strong eat up the Weak." Japan invaded China in 1894 and stunned the world with its defeat of the continental giant. China ceded Taiwan and other territories, paid a large indemnity, and gave Japan unequal diplomatic and commercial privileges.

The western powers, however, were protective of the white-members-only imperialist club and forced non-white Japan to give up the territorial gains. The humiliated Japan learned this new lesson as well. While twentieth century Japanese aggression against China, Korea, the Philippines and eventually Pearl Harbor had many causes, its desire to be a rich, powerful, and respected nation had nineteenth century roots in the western way to have the goods through might makes right.[15]

On the personal level, Having the Goods gets ugly when we think like a certain rich man in a story told by Jesus. The rich man had taken stock. His barns were overflowing from the harvest. "What shall I do?" He answered his own question. "I will build bigger barns and fill them up. Then I can rest, eat, drink, be merry!" Jesus finished the story with a warning. "But God said to him, 'You fool! What if you died this night?'" (Luke 12:16-21). It is not nice to call people names. Jesus taught that calling someone a fool makes one liable to the fires of Gehenna. Yet God himself called the rich man a fool. Why?

Ask, "How does the sun go around the earth?" and answers vary from a chariot pulling it across the sky to a great turning wheel. Unlike the ancients, we know that the correct question is, "How does the earth go around the sun?" Ask the wrong question, you get the wrong answer. The rich man asked the wrong question, "What shall I do with my overflowing harvest?" He asked himself and not God. He was a fool. He thought he was a good person because he had good things. He did not concern himself with God.

One of the questions a financial planner asks is, "Are you prepared for retirement?" That is a good question if retirement is your goal. Like the rich man's question, though, this question is short-sighted. What does it profit a person to gain the whole world – a comfortable retirement, nice clothes, vacation cruises – and lose his soul? The better question is, "Are you prepared for heaven?" If not, see your spiritual planner!

Born in 1920, Tom White served in WWII and won a chest full of medals including the silver star. He came home and took over his father's failing construction business and built it into the largest construction firm in Boston. As a millionaire, his goal was to die penniless. He steadily gave away his wealth by selling his company, his assets, and his house to continue supporting Partners in Health, a leader in medical care in Haiti and the Third World.

Paul English, the founder of the travel website Kayak, became interested in philanthropy and heard about Tom. He looked him up and met him for lunch at a nice Boston restaurant.

"So I read about this group you're with, Partners in Health, that has been working in Haiti twenty years and how you guys raised thirty million for it," said Paul. He added, "But twenty million, I heard came from you."

Tom blushed and looked down at his napkin. "Oh, I don't know about that."

Paul grinned at him. "I bet you think that makes you a good person. I think it makes you a shitty fundraiser." Tom threw back his head and laughed at the ceiling.[16]

They became friends. Paul English visited Tom monthly at his apartment over gin and tonic. Paul gave one million dollars to Partners in Health. He backstopped an expensive vaccine for cholera following the 2010 earthquake, which saved many lives and made the vaccine more available and affordable around the world. When Tom died in 2011, Paul joined the board of Partners in Health. Tom White gave his fortune for the medical care of people in Haiti. Paul English caught the philanthropy bug and got others to give. It was a virtuous circle unconcerned with Having the Goods. In the end, the rich man Tom White got his wish. He died nearly penniless on earth, rich in heaven.

Reflection Questions

1. When have I believed that achieving one more goal, gaining one more advantage, or securing one more possession would finally make me happy – and what actually happened?
2. In what ways do I measure my worth by my productivity, success, reputation, or financial stability, and how does that affect my inner peace?
3. How are you, like the rich man with a great harvest, preparing for retirement and how are you, like Tom White, preparing for heaven?

Scripture Verse

"Better a little with tranquility than a great deal with striving and chasing after the wind." – *Ecclesiastes 4:6*

Action Steps

1. Create a Daily Gratitude List – But Focus on What You Already Have

At the end of the day, list three things for which you are grateful. Make sure that at least one item is not connected to achievement or material comfort but to relationship, character, or insight – such as a meaningful conversation, a moment of clarity, or a challenge that helped you grow. This gradually reorients your heart toward what is already abundant rather than what is missing.

2. Fast From One Area of Striving for Seven Days

Choose one form of striving – staying late at work, comparing yourself to others online, or constantly planning the next accomplishment – and pause that behavior for a week. Notice the emotional response when you are not actively "getting ahead." The discomfort or relief that appears will reveal how deeply achievement shapes your identity.

3. Begin or End the Day With Five Minutes of Stillness

Sit quietly in a place free from distractions and screens. Breathe slowly. Let your mind settle, and allow thoughts about success, productivity, or status to rise and pass without chasing them. Gently ask for clarity about what truly matters today and the courage to release pressures that don't serve your well-being. Over time, stillness creates space for peace rather than performance.

Relevant Citations from the Catechism of the Catholic Church

1. **CCC 2424** – Warns against reducing human worth to economic success or treating people as instruments of profit.

2. **CCC 2547** – Teaches that true happiness is found not in material abundance but in spiritual freedom and detachment.
3. **CCC 1723** – Explains that worldly achievements and pleasures cannot satisfy the human heart; only a deeper good can.

St. Thomas More (16th century)

Patron saint of: lawyers, civil servants, integrity in public life. More reached the height of political success as Lord Chancellor of England. Yet he discovered that status cannot secure peace if it costs one's integrity. He chose truth over power, revealing the emptiness of achievement divorced from conscience.

St. Josephine Bakhita (19th–20th century)

Patron saint of: Sudan, survivors of human trafficking. Though she lived much of her early life without freedom, status, or possessions, Bakhita radiated joy and dignity. Her serenity even as a slave did not come from "having the goods" but from an identity rooted beyond circumstance. She embodies freedom from the illusion that external success defines us.

St. Óscar Romero (20th century)

Patron saint of: El Salvador, social justice, voices for the voiceless. Initially cautious and career-oriented, Romero experienced a profound shift when he witnessed injustice and suffering. He moved from personal advancement to courageous advocacy, ultimately giving his life for truth. His transformation shows that real fulfillment lies not in achievement but in aligning one's life with compassion and justice.

What Makes Us Happier?
LEVEL THREE
Doing Good

Doing Good: The Good

In the 1960 version of The Game of Life boardgame, you drive along the road of life in a little pink, blue, red, or green plastic car. You get married, hit payday, pay taxes, and choose what kind of house to live in. If you are wise, you buy insurance because with a flick of the spinner there is a lot of chance in life. At the end of the game is the Day of Reckoning. It has nothing to do with standing before the judgment seat of God. The winner of the Game of Life is the player who has the most money.

A few generations later, the makers of The Game of Life made some changes. Your little plastic car can land on squares such as "adopt a pet" and "say no to drugs" and "feed the homeless." The new and improved goal is to retire with the most Life Points and win the game of life. The updated version of The Game of Life shifted the goal line from Having the Goods to Doing Good.

A scholar of the law asked Jesus, "What must I do to inherit eternal life?" (Luke 10:25-37). Our question, "What makes us happier?" is a version of his question. How do I live a good life? How do I win the game of life? (In the gospel of Mark, the rich young man asked the same question. Jesus replied, "Go, sell all you have and give to the poor." Can we spin again?)

To the scholar, Jesus asked his own question, "What does Scripture say?" The scholar gave the answer straight from the Bible, "Love God and love neighbor." To win the game of life and inherit eternal life, we must love God and neighbor. But who is our neighbor? The comedian and misanthrope W. C. Fields was caught reading the Bible on a movie set to which he responded, "I'm looking for loopholes." The scholar of the law in the Bible wanted to make sure he understood the fine print. He asked Jesus, "Who is my neighbor?"

Who is my neighbor? Who must I love? Jesus replied with a story about a Jewish pilgrim beaten by robbers, avoided by a passing priest and Levite, and eventually helped by a Good Samaritan (Luke 10:25-37). Martin Luther King Jr. observed that the priest and Levite asked themselves this question. "If I stop to help this man, what will happen to me?" The priest and Levite might have suspected the bandits were hiding in ambush. Even if it was safe, getting involved was not convenient and would upset their plans for that day. There was unknown cost. Surely the authorities had more resources to deal with this unfortunate situation. Besides, the pilgrim should have known better than to travel alone. "If I stop to help this man, what will happen to me?" Reverend King did not stop there. "But then the good Samaritan came by, and he reversed the question: 'If I do not stop to help this man, what will happen to him?'" Instead of asking

Level Three – Doing Good

the question, "What will happen to me?" the Samaritan asked the question, "What will happen to him?"[17]

King made the question his own. He walked the talk. In Memphis in 1968, garbage workers were on strike. King must have wondered, "If I do not stop to help the sanitation workers in Memphis, what will happen to them?" King went to Memphis to support them, and it was there he was assassinated.

The answer to "What makes us happier?" leads us beyond Feeling Good and Having the Goods to another question, "What if I do not stop?" If we do not stop to help mothers and their unborn children, what will happen to them? If we do not stop to help migrants and refugees, what will happen to them? If we do not stop to help our polluted planet and thousands of species going extinct, what will happen to our grandchildren's grandchildren? Doing Good for others as the Good Samaritan did starts with a question, "What if I don't stop?"

Who must we stop for? In Jesus' day, Samaritans and Jews held each other in contempt and had nothing to do with each other. To the Jews, a "Good Samaritan" was an oxymoron like a Good Roman Legionnaire. Making a Samaritan more righteous than a holy priest or learned Levite challenged the categories of who was worth stopping for. If Jesus told the story today, the Good Samaritan would be a cat and the robbers' victim a dog. We can imagine other unlikely pairings: If you are black, it's those who are white. If you speak English, it's those who speak Spanish. If you live in the suburbs, it's the Mexicans with the leafblowers making our lawns look nice. If you are an American citizen, it's the illegal immigrant. If you are Christian, it's the Muslim. If you are straight, it's the gays. If you are me, it's the people who are nothing but trouble.

When we stop and do good, human suffering becomes bearable and even redeemed. Saint Pope John Paul II wrote a beautiful reflection, "On the Christian Meaning of Human Suffering." He gave the story of the Good Samaritan as example. Going beyond sympathy and compassion, the Samaritan freely gave his time, money, and self for his suffering sworn enemy. John Paul II added that society itself is at its finest when its medical institutions, education systems, and social work follow the example of the Good Samaritan and are structured in answer to the question, "What will happen to the least among us if we do not stop?"[18]

What must I do to inherit eternal life? How do I win the game of life? What makes me happier? They say, "Don't ask a question if you don't want to know the answer." One question leads to another. "Who is my neighbor?" leads to, "What will happen to them if you do not stop?" Wasn't it nicer to think that the Good Samaritan story was all about being helpful to strangers and moving on?[19]

Doing Good: The Bad

When Scotty Scheffler tapped in for par on the final hole, he won the 2025 British Open golf tournament. He made it all look so routine. But then he saw his family. He thrust both arms into the air, pumped his fists, and tossed his cap into the air. His 15-month-old son Bennett tried to walk up a slope to the 18th green toward his dad with the claret jug trophy only to face-plant. At the press conference, Scotty Scheffler reflected that the celebration of a tournament win lasted only a few minutes before it was on to the next one. He loved the work required to be the best. He thrived on the competition. But in terms of fulfillment, he questioned why he wanted to win so badly when the thrill of winning was fleeting. For the 29-year-old from Texas, his family was the real thrill.[20] Like Scotty Scheffler in our pursuit of happiness, Ground Zero for Doing Good is the family.

Family is not just important to our happiness. The family is important to society. As strong healthy cells make a strong healthy body, strong healthy families make a strong healthy society. The Catholic church supports policies for strong healthy families – a living wage where only one parent needs to work to put food on the table while the spouse can stay home and raise the children, health insurance that does not force a choice between a visit to the doctor and paying the rent, and immigration reform that unites families rather than separates and deports their members. Extended families, blended families, grandparents raising grandkids, and many other kinds of families make a strong healthy society. Family is not just important to families. The family is important to the world.

The Sunday after Christmas Day, the Catholic church celebrates the Feast of the Holy Family of Jesus, Mary and Joseph. On the feast of the Holy Family, we expect to hear Scripture praise the family. But the Church gives us instead the story of Hannah.

The prayer of the barren Hannah had been heard. She conceived a son. After Hannah weaned her infant, she took him to the temple. Hannah said to Eli the old priest, "I prayed for this child, and the LORD granted my request. Now I, in turn, give him to the LORD; as long as he lives, he shall be dedicated to the LORD" (1 Samuel 1:27-28). That's when she did it. She gave her only child to Eli the old priest. In a basket covered with a goat skin plus a bag of flour, she handed him over and departed. The mother went home without her son. Hannah left Samuel there.

What kind of mother is she? What mother would abandon her only son to the care of an old priest? What mother would leave her future in a basket on the temple step?

The feast of the Holy Family defies the notion that the family is the end all and be all. It points beyond the joy we receive when we do good for our family towards an even greater good awaiting us. Politicians from time to time talk about Family Values. They make it sound like Family Values is a book in the Bible. It is not. The Bible has Gospel Values. And the first Gospel Value is to put God first. The Lord gave us the Ten Commandments. The First Commandment is, "You shall not have other gods besides me" (Exodus 20:3). In other words, "Put God first." True, the Fourth Commandment is important. "Honor your father and your mother" (Exodus 20:12). We are to take care of family. But the first commandment is first. Put God first.

Ask a pregnant mom and dad, "Is it a boy or girl?" If they like surprises, they will say, "We don't know, as long as the child is *healthy*." Ask a mom and dad proud about their growing child, "What do you think your child will do when she grows up?" They will reply, "We don't care, as long as she is *happy*." A happy, healthy child. What more could mom and dad want?

Christmas is the family season. Retailers call it the holiday season, religious folk say it is the Christmas season, but without a doubt, Christmas is the family season. We make great efforts through planes, trains, and automobiles to be with family even if only for a day or two. Christmas time is hard for those who have suffered a death in the family or a divorce. Christmas reminds us how important the family is. Yet the name of the Church feast day square in the middle of the Christmas season is not what we expect. The Church does not celebrate the Feast of the Healthy Family. We do not celebrate the Feast of the Happy Family. We celebrate the Feast of the Holy Family.

What does it mean to be holy? The chalice is the cup used at the altar during the Mass for the consecration of the wine. The paten is the plate or bowl for the consecration of the bread. The chalice and paten, once blessed, are used only for Mass. They are not used for coffee and donuts. They have been set apart for God. They are holy.

The Feast of the Holy Family makes clear that Jesus was born into a family. His mother was Mary. Her husband was Joseph. Without a doubt, God thinks the family is good. Yet the family is not an end in itself. The purpose of the family is to set us apart for God. The family helps make us holy.

In the daily grind of family life, stuck with these sisters and brothers and parents and cousins that we did not choose, we learn to give ourselves to one another. Families teach us to put others before self. In families we learn to put God first. When Father Jorge Torres was the Director of Vocations for the Diocese of Orlando, he would speak at parishes about where priests come from. "I don't want your money. I want your first born." In other words, families are not an end in themselves. They help us serve God and his purposes.

Level Three – Doing Good

One mother, checking on her six boys after she had put them to bed, said a nightly prayer. "Thank you, God, for these boys you entrusted to us." She and her husband recognized that the kids were only on loan. They belonged to the Lord. Thirty years later, the boys had grown into married men. They gave her and her husband seventeen grandkids, all baptized. Five of their six boys were active in the Church. Their family had done its job to help them become holy.

At this point I would like to say, "Put God first and everything will be okay." For Hannah, it was. After leaving Samuel at the temple, she went on to have three more sons and two daughters. I wish I could say "put God first" and your money worries will go away, a great job paying good money will come along, and your health will be restored. But there is no guarantee what will happen.

For the family who put God first above all, life became hard. Mary said yes to the angel Gabriel to become the mother of God, and, unmarried and pregnant, came close to being stoned to death. Joseph, saying yes to the angel and taking the pregnant Mary into his home, lost his reputation as a righteous god-fearing man. Mary and Joseph gave birth to Jesus not in a nice hospital or in a warm home with family but in a barn surrounded by dirty animals and strangers. They had to flee for their lives in the middle of the night when King Herod tried to kill the rumored newborn king of the Jews. They were refugees in Egypt for two years until Herod died. For the holy family who put God first above all else, life for their little family did not become easier. Life became harder.

Hannah left Samuel there. There's more to the story. Samuel grew up in the temple. He became a priest and prophet. Samuel was the one sent by the Lord to anoint a shepherd boy and make him king. King David established the Kingdom of Israel. His reign gave hope to the people of God. They looked forward to a future Son of David to establish the reign of God. It would be fulfilled a thousand years later with the birth of Jesus which we celebrate at Christmas. All this happened because Hannah left Samuel there.

Doing Good: The Ugly

History is littered with examples where good people set out to do good yet harvested great evil.

During the 19th and 20th century, the U.S. federal government sought to assimilate Native American tribes. Government boarding schools separated many indigenous children from their families and forced them to abandon their own language, dress, customs, and even names. Of the more than 400 boarding schools, 87 were run by Catholic entities.[21] While many Church-run boarding schools sheltered orphans and provided formal education, the system itself left a legacy of trauma, racism, poverty, addiction, and suicide.[22] Pope Francis traveled in 2022 to Canada and apologized to the indigenous tribes. "I want to tell you how very sorry I am and to ask for forgiveness for the evil perpetrated by not a few Catholics.[23] "Do good" did great evil to countless indigenous people.

For generations, meaningful action against child sexual abuse by Catholic clergy and personnel was trumped by the fear of scandal. Church leaders were concerned that scandalized church members would lose faith in the Church and God. Following the best practices of the day, some abusers made a good confession and got a new start at another parish assignment. Some were sent for psychological evaluation and in-patient treatment. In 2002, the United States bishops enacted a zero tolerance policy. They mandated accountability and transparency to put the protection of children and youth first. In 2024, the Catholic church in the United States conducted 2.2 million background checks on clergy, employees, and volunteers; five million adults, youth, and children received training to identify and report abuse. After more than two decades of Church efforts to protect children, 146 new reports of abuse were made in 2024 and 1,434 victim-survivors and families received continued support.[24] Even one new case of abuse is one case too many. But progress has been made.

Some say that religion causes more harm than good. They cite the religious wars of the medieval period, the Crusades, and church-sanctioned colonialism. As murderous as these events were, regimes without religion make the case for religion. By one estimate, Communist China killed and starved seventy-six million of its citizens in a mere forty years (1949-1987), the Soviet Union killed sixty-two million in its seventy years' reign (1917-87), and Nazi Germany killed twenty-one million including six million Jews.[25] I doubt that Karl Marx woke up one day with the thought, "How can I devise an atheist ideology in which governments slaughter tens of millions of their own citizens?" Yet, however well-meant, Marx's political theory in response to the great suffering brought on by 19th century industrialization did just that. Doing Good can lead to great evil.

Our own frustration with the way our efforts to do good end up badly can be summed up by Saint Paul. "The willing is ready at hand, but doing the good is not. For I do not do the good I want, but I do the evil I do not want" (Romans 7:18-19). We can relate to his misery. The human condition is one where we want to do good yet end up doing evil. Paul owned how he could do good in the sight of the world yet still accomplish nothing. Preceding his "Love is patient, love is kind" tribute favored at weddings, Paul wondered at the futility of his efforts alone. "If I speak in human and angelic tongues but do not have love, I am a resounding gong or a clashing cymbal. And if I have the gift of prophecy and comprehend all mysteries and all knowledge; if I have all faith so as to move mountains but do not have love, I am nothing. If I give away everything I own, and if I hand my body over so that I may boast but do not have love, I gain nothing" (1 Corinthians 13:1-3).

One more example how Doing Good can get ugly.

The Pharisees appear in the scriptures as opponents of Jesus. While modern eyes see them as "holier-than-thou" hypocrites who loved money and seats of honor and power over the people, they were actually a reform movement seeking to resist Roman assimilation. The Romans had conquered Israel and expected the people to work hard and pay Roman taxes. To assimilate the

Jewish people into the Roman empire, the Romans promoted worship of Roman gods, counted time and seasons according to the Roman calendar, and used Roman names. The Pharisees took a stand against Romanization. To remain faithful to the Jewish covenant, the Pharisees held fast to kosher laws, Sabbath regulations, and worship in the Jerusalem temple. Hence healing on the Sabbath or eating unclean foods was more than a difference of opinion. Such actions let the camel's nose slip under the tent, compromising the covenant with God and inviting Roman assimilation.[26]

The Pharisees as depicted in the New Testament were principled religious men well-regarded by the people. They probably knew the scriptures better than anyone in their day and faithfully followed the letter of the law. In their effort to do good and resist Roman assimilation, they ended up allying with their enemy, the Roman governor Pontius Pilate. Tragically, they collaborated in the arrest and crucifixion of Jesus, the very one who came to forge the new and eternal covenant with God.

Reflection Questions

1. When have I, like the Good Samaritan, stopped to help someone? What happened? What did it cost me? Was it worth it?

2. "In families we learn to put God first." What do I think about this statement? How have I seen it practiced (or not practiced) in my family?

3. Saint Paul lamented that he did not do the good he wanted and instead did the evil he did not want. His good intention and strong willpower did not carry the day. When have I set out to do good and instead ended up adding to misery?

Scripture Verse

"Learn to do good. Seek justice, rescue the oppressed, defend the orphan, plead for the widow." – *Isaiah 1:17*

Action Steps

1. Create a Daily Gratitude List – Focused on Goodness Received and Goodness Given

Each day this week, write down three things for which you are grateful. Include one moment when someone extended goodness toward you, and another moment – no matter how small – when you helped someone else. This trains the heart to notice goodness as a shared exchange rather than a one-way effort.

2. Fast From One Form of Indifference for Seven Days

Choose a pattern that keeps you from seeing others clearly – scrolling past people's struggles online, pretending not to notice someone overwhelmed, or avoiding a person whose needs feel heavy. Pause that behavior for one week. Notice how compassion rises when you allow yourself to see people rather than avoid them.

3. Begin or End the Day with Five Minutes of Stillness on the Theme of "Who Is My Neighbor?"

Sit quietly and review your day in your mind's eye. Let the faces of those you encountered come to you – especially the ones you overlooked. Ask for clarity to see others more honestly and courage to respond when compassion invites you forward. Over time, this stillness expands your inner readiness to do good.

Relevant Citations from the Catechism of the Catholic Church

1. **CCC 2447** – The works of mercy – spiritual and material – are essential expressions of love for our neighbor
2. **CCC** 1931 – Every person has inherent dignity, which demands justice and the protection of the vulnerable.

LEVEL THREE – DOING GOOD

3. **CCC 1829** – Charity is shown in concrete actions toward others, especially the most vulnerable.

St. Vincent de Paul (17th century)

Patron saint of: charitable societies, volunteers, caregivers of the poor. Vincent poured his life into serving orphans, prisoners, the sick, and the forgotten. He treated every suffering person as a personal invitation to love. His life shows how consistently choosing to "stop" for others creates a legacy of compassion that outlives us.

St. Teresa of Calcutta (20th century)

Patron saint of: World Youth Day, missionaries of charity, those seeking to serve the poorest. Mother Teresa stepped into the places the world ignored – streets where the dying lay, orphanages without resources, neighborhoods marked by disease and rejection. She believed that every person deserved to be seen and loved. Her life demonstrates how doing good often begins with the simplest moment of recognizing someone's dignity.

St. Maximilian Kolbe (20th century)

Patron saint of: prisoners, families, those struggling with addiction. Imprisoned in Auschwitz, Kolbe volunteered to die in place of another prisoner – a husband and father who cried out that he did not want to be separated from his family. Kolbe's act of sacrificial love embodies the deepest truth of the Good Samaritan story: real goodness costs something, and real compassion asks not "What will happen to me?" but "What will happen to them?"

What Makes Us Happiest?
Level Four
God Is Good

The classic TV animated show "A Charlie Brown Christmas" opens with the kids skating on a frozen lake. Linus and Charlie Brown head to the lake to join the skating but first stop for a chat at the red brick wall.

"I think there must be something wrong with me, Linus." Charlie Brown frowns. "Christmas is coming, but I'm not happy. I don't feel the way I'm supposed to feel."

It bugs Charlie Brown when Snoopy enters his doghouse in a Christmas decorating contest not for the beauty of Christmas lights but to win a cash prize. Lucy complains that all she ever gets at Christmas are "stupid toys or clothes or a bicycle." What she really wants is "real estate." Meanwhile, Charlie Brown's little sister Sally writes to Santa that if gifts are too much trouble, "make it easy on yourself, just send money." When Charlie Brown challenges her wish list, Sally explains with her absolute innocence, "All I want is what's coming to me. All I want is my fair share."

Charlie Brown was no blockhead. Something was wrong with Christmas. These things would not make him happy. Would anything make Charlie Brown happy?

God is Good: The Good

Our culture tells us that when we are comfortable and in good health, we'll be happy. Jesus lived homeless with only a rock for a pillow. He depended completely on the generosity of others for his daily bread.

Our culture tells us that when we have the things we want, we'll be happy. Jesus was born poor, lived poor, and died poor. On the cross, he had nothing to his name except his tunic, and the Roman soldiers took that away from him.

Our culture tells us that when we have a good reputation, the respect of important people, lines of followers on social media, and a few real friends above all, we'll be happy. Jesus, hanging naked at a public crossroads, was spat upon by the good people of his day, mocked by a criminal crucified near him, and abandoned by his few friends.

Our culture tells us that when we have the freedom to do what we want, we'll be happy. Jesus the Christ was nailed fast on wood. On the cross, the almighty Lord who made the heavens and earth and the seas could not move.

Yet Jesus could say, "All this I have told you so that my joy may be in you and your joy may be complete" (John 15:11). What in the world was he talking about?

We can answer that question with another question. What does Feeling Good, Having the Goods, and Doing Good all have in common? The Good! Our pursuit of happiness is really the desire for the Good. As the earlier sections described, our pursuits of happiness cannot deliver lasting happiness. They can lead us only so far. In fact, when we pursue Feeling Good, Having the Goods, and even Doing Good, we become miserable. Why is this?

"The desire for God is written on the human heart," the *Catechism of the Catholic Church* teaches. We desire the Good because we desire God. Why do we desire God? Because God is good. "Only in God will we find the truth and happiness that we never stop searching for" (paragraph 27). Or as Saint Augustine wrote, "You have made us for yourself, and our heart is restless until it rests in you." God made us to share in his own divine life. All of our desires and pursuits are good insofar as they lead us to God. God, who is goodness itself, is what the human heart desires.

How do we get what our heart truly desires? Here's the bad news. We can't. We can't get there from here. Feeling Good, Having the Goods, and Doing Good are what we do. We can do the things that make us feel good. We can achieve so that we have the goods. We can serve others and do good. By relying only on ourselves, however, we fall short. We cannot get what our heart truly desires.

We are like Charlie Brown. Frustrated at the rehearsal of the school Christmas play, he cried out, "I guess I really don't know what Christmas is all about. Isn't there anyone who knows what Christmas is all about?"

His buddy Linus stepped up. "Sure, Charlie Brown, I can tell you what Christmas is all about. Lights please?" A single spotlight shone down on Linus. He put down his blanket and recited the story from the gospel of Luke:

"Now there were shepherds in that region living in the fields and keeping the night watch over their flock. The angel of the Lord appeared to them and the glory of the Lord shone around them, and they were struck with great fear. The angel said to them, 'Do not be afraid; for behold, I proclaim to you good news of great joy that will be for all the people. For today in the city of David a savior has been born for you who is Christ and Lord. And this will be a sign for you: you will find an infant wrapped in swaddling clothes and lying in a manger.' And suddenly there was a multitude of the heavenly host with the angel, praising God and saying: 'Glory to God in the highest and on earth peace to those on whom his favor rests'." Linus picked up his blanket and walked back to Charlie Brown. "That's what Christmas is all about, Charlie Brown."

The Good News is that God does for us what we cannot do for ourselves. He gives us our heart's desire. He gives us himself.

A mother had her little boy help set up their ceramic nativity scene. As she unwrapped a figurine in blue from its bubble wrap, she asked, "Who is this?"

"Mary," the boy replied.

"That's right, Mary, the mother of Jesus." The mother placed the Mary figurine next to the empty manger.

"Who is this?" She held up a little man holding a walking staff.

"Joseph."

"That's right, Joseph, the husband of Mary." The mother placed the Joseph figurine next to Mary in the midst of shepherds and sheep.

Last of all, the mother unwrapped the smallest figurine. It was the only piece that would fit in the empty manger. "Who is this?"

The boy's eyes grew wide. "Breakable."

The Christmas carol, "What Child Is This" sung to the tune "Greensleeves" begins innocently enough. "What child is this / Who's laid to rest / On Mary's lap is sleeping?" A later verse rarely sung continues, "Nails, spear shall pierce Him through / The cross be borne for me, for you / Hail, hail the Word made flesh / The Babe, the Son of Mary." God gave us himself in Jesus Christ. He became breakable. Nails and spear pierced him through. He bore the cross for me and you. He has freed us from our captivity to our fruitless pursuit of Feeling Good, Having the Goods, and Doing Good. The Lord has freed us for abundant joy in him.

When a bride and groom marry, they stand before the altar and make a promise. They promise to be true to each other in good times and in bad, in sickness and health, all the days of their lives. They promise to give themselves completely and without condition to the other person until death separates them.

With the birth of Jesus Christ, God fulfilled his promise to us. He had promised to be true to us in good times and in bad, in sickness and health, all the days of our lives. Heaven and earth were joined, the two became one, through the incarnation of Jesus Christ. God kept his promise to give himself completely and without condition to us. Not even death will separate us from God. As beautiful as Christmas is with its manger scene and caroling and shepherds and pageantry, its real beauty is God's promise realized in Jesus Christ. Jesus the Savior born on Christmas was crucified on Good Friday. Then something amazing happened. On Easter Sunday morning, the tomb was empty. "On the third day he rose again."

God is Good: The Bad

Taylor Swift delivered the 2022 commencement speech for New York University at Yankee Stadium. She offered "some life hacks I wish I knew when I was starting out." Her life hacks included reminders that "life can be heavy," to "learn to live alongside cringe," and to "never be ashamed of trying."

At the Last Supper with his followers, Jesus had some final words before going to the cross. Taking off the training wheels, he did not give a life hack. He gave a command. "Love one another as I love you" (John 15:12).

This commandment, "Love one another as I love you," makes Catholics different from other people. Not just that we come to Mass every Sunday morning while many folks catch up on their sleep or hit the beach. What is different is that we do not set the bar.

Our culture tells us, "You decide if they are illegal aliens trying to take our jobs or undocumented immigrants forced to flee their homeland. You decide if it is an unborn baby or a choice. In short, you decide who to love and how to love. You decide what is best for you. You decide."

Catholics are different. We do not decide who to love or how to love. Jesus set the bar. He said, "Love one another as I love you." The key word is "as."

How did he love? Humbly, he washed feet and nobly carried the cross. Who did he love? Friends who ran away in his hour of need. Soldiers who whipped him and mocked him and drove spikes into his hands and feet. He loved even Judas who betrayed him to the authorities.

Another way that Catholics are different from everyone else is that we love not just our friends and families. After all, the word "catholic" means "universal." It's not about me. It's about we. Someone compared the earth to a spaceship in flight in which one of the three astronauts on board is consuming eighty-five percent of the resources on the spaceship and is plotting to secure the remaining fifteen percent as well. The comparison is strong stuff for us who have not only a house for ourselves but a house for our car. It hits close to home for us who drink unlimited clean water and likely swim in a ten-thousand-gallon pool. Who would dare compare us to the selfish astronaut? Father Rainero Cantalamessa, the Papal Preacher for forty years, that's who. Catholics consider not only our immediate family and friends. Everyone from the pew to the pope must ask the difficult question, "How will this help people who are poor?" When we fail to love as Jesus has loved us, we go to confession but we do not lower the bar.

When we are so different from everyone else, people notice. And it's not always good. Many criticized Pope Francis for speaking strongly about human activity driving climate change and pollution. He did not lower the bar. Instead, he met with Bono from the rock band U2 in a public meeting to talk about climate change. Many criticize the Catholic Church's stand against abortion. Rather than lowering the bar, the Church funds pregnancy clinics and healing ministries such as Project Rachel. It walks with mothers and families in need, promotes alternatives to abortion, and seeks to create a culture of life from womb to tomb. The Catholic church teaches that all lives matter. From womb to tomb, mothers and their unborn children, refugees and immigrants, black and white, gay and straight, every person has God-given dignity. "Love one another as I love you."

Here's the choice: do what feels good, do what gets the goods, do good as you see best, and be like everyone else. Or, be different. Be Catholic. "Love one another as I love you," even when people notice and not in a favorable sense. You can't have it both ways. Only one way leads to true joy.

When you love completely and forget yourself, you find joy. Don't take my word for it. Get to know the joyful men and women who chose to be different. The saints staked their lives on what Jesus promised, "All this I have told you so that my joy may be in you and your joy may be complete" (John 15:11).

LEVEL FOUR – GOD IS GOOD

God is Good: The Ugly

Adam and Eve were more than happy. They had everything they could want. There was no death or pain or shame. They were in paradise! In the cool of the evening, the Lord God himself walked with them. They were friends with God. Warning them only not to take from the tree of the knowledge of good and evil, the Lord gave them everything else in the garden to have as their own. What could possibly go wrong?

The serpent slid close to the woman. "Did God really say, 'You shall not eat from any of the trees in the garden'?" Notice how the serpent turned God's warning about one tree into a "No trespassing" sign on all the trees.

The woman gamely corrected the record. "We may eat of the fruit of the trees in the garden; it is only about the fruit of the tree in the middle of the garden that God said, 'You shall not eat it or even touch it, or else you will die.'" You go, girl!

The serpent was no quitter. It struck. "You certainly will not die! God knows well that when you eat of it your eyes will be opened and you will be like gods, who know good and evil." The serpent's claim raised some tempting questions. Who would not want to be like gods? Why not decide for yourself what is good and evil? Why let God set the rules? Who needs such a God? In just a few words, the serpent planted doubt in the heart.

Not doubt in the existence of God but doubt in the goodness of God. Did God really want our good? Did he want us to be his friends and share his happiness? Or did God want to limit out freedom?

That tree looked good. Gaining wisdom was certainly a good thing. What tipped the scales was that the woman and man doubted the goodness of God. They trusted the serpent more than the Lord God. So the woman took some of the fruit of the tree and ate it, and so did her husband.

The story of Adam and Eve is our story. Something in us wants to be God. We want to decide for ourselves what is right and wrong. We want to be able to make ourselves happy. In our hearts, we doubt the goodness of God. As Bishop Barron has said numerous times, we see God as a petty tyrant. Our inner Adam resents this twisted version of God. No wonder we rebel. We fall for Satan's trap in Milton's "Paradise Lost," "Better to reign in hell than serve in heaven."

Humankind has taken the forbidden fruit and proved the serpent partly right. The eyes of both the man and woman were opened. But they did not become like gods. Just the opposite! They were so ashamed that they hid in the bushes from the Lord God when he came in the cool of the evening to walk with them. No longer friends with God, they were afraid of him.

The story gets worse. Playing hide-and-seek with the Lord was a losing proposition. The Lord God quickly found them hiding in the bushes. He asked, "What happened?"

Adam was quick to point a finger at Eve. "The woman whom you put here with me," (backhanding God for the unfortunate events) "gave me the fruit." Eve was no better. "The serpent tricked me." She neatly placed the blame on the snake which, by the way, God had allowed into the garden.

What was worse? That Adam and Eve wanted to be like gods? That they were afraid of the Lord God? That they blamed others? The temptation of Adam and Eve went badly. Paradise became purgatory. The serpent had lied through its fangs. They did die. (Genesis 3:8-13).

What did the Lord God do about this terrible turn?

In the fourth century, a man named Jerome lived in Bethlehem. He was a scripture scholar. He translated the Hebrew and Greek scriptures into Latin, which became the Bible used by the Catholic Church for the next thousand years.

One Christmas night, Jerome was praying and thinking about the birth of Jesus. Suddenly the Christ child appeared to him in dazzling light. "Jerome," asked the Christ child, "what are you going to give me for my birthday?"

"Baby Jesus," said Jerome, "I give you my heart."

"Yes, but give me something more."

"I give you all that I have and all that I am."

"There is still something more that I want."

"Divine infant, I have nothing more. What is it that I can give you?"

"Jerome, give me your sins. Give me your sins that I may pardon all of them."

And the great Saint Jerome wept for joy.

At Christmas, we exchange gifts. We take a present from under the Christmas tree and give it to the person we bought it for. "I hope you like it." They in turn give you a gift. "Merry Christmas."

God gave us a gift. You can't find it on Amazon. You can't make it. God gave us his only Son. While we were still sinners and not admitting our fault, he suffered and died for us. He took our shame upon himself. Unlike Adam and Eve in the Garden of Eden, Jesus was obedient to God the Father in the Garden of Gethsemane. He trusted God with his life even to the cross.

What do we give to God in exchange for such a gift? Our sins. Our secrets. Our shame. We give him even our doubt in his goodness. We give it all to God in the Sacrament of Reconciliation. He nails them to the cross. He gives us his pardon and peace. He gives us his hand in friendship. We walk again with the Lord and the way to true happiness lies before us.

At Nativity Catholic Church where I am the pastor, the saying, "Where every day is Christmas," is more than words. It is how we become happiest.

Reflection Questions

1. In what ways do I sense like Charlie Brown that something deeper is missing from feeling good, having the goods, and even doing good?
2. How has the command "Love one another as I love you" made a difference in whom I love and how I love?
3. "We want to be able to make ourselves happy. In our hearts, we doubt the goodness of God." When have I doubted that God truly desires my good?

Scripture Verse

"Taste and see that the Lord is good; blessed is the one who takes refuge in him." – *Psalm 34:9*

Action Steps

1. Create a Daily Gratitude List – Focused on Moments of Goodness Breaking Through

Write down three things each day this week for which you are grateful, making sure at least one reflects a gift of goodness – an unexpected kindness, a moment of peace, a sense of being guided, or a surprising insight. This opens the heart to the possibility that goodness is something given, not merely earned.

2. Fast From One Form of Self-Reliance for Seven Days

Choose one habit of overcontrol – constant planning, perfectionism, rehearsing anxieties, or micromanaging outcomes – and surrender it for a week. Notice what rises when you stop trying to hold everything together. This practice reveals both the limits of self-reliance and the comfort that comes from letting go.

3. Begin or End the Day With Five Minutes of Stillness on the Theme "What Goodness Came to Me Today?"

Sit in silence and slowly review your day. Instead of focusing on what you achieved, ask how goodness appeared – through a person, an experience, a moment of clarity, or quiet reassurance. Let yourself receive these moments rather than analyzing them. This practice shifts the heart from striving to trust.

Relevant Citations from the Catechism of the Catholic Church

1. CCC 27 – The desire for God is written in the human heart because we are created to share in His life.
2. CCC 396–398 – Humanity's first sin came from doubting God's goodness.

3. **CCC 457** – Christ came to reconcile us with God and reveal God's goodness and love.

St. Hildegard of Bingen (12th century)

Patron saint of: musicians, writers, natural scientists. Hildegard experienced profound visions of God's goodness expressed through creation, beauty, music, and healing. She believed that the world pulses with God's life-giving vitality – what she called *viriditas*, or "the greening power." Her life teaches that God's goodness is not abstract but vibrantly alive in the world around us.

St. Edith Stein (St. Teresa Benedicta of the Cross) (20th century)

Patron saint of: Europe, philosophers, those seeking truth. Edith Stein was a brilliant philosopher and a seeker who journeyed through atheism before encountering God as the fullness of truth and goodness. Even in the face of rising hatred and suffering, she trusted in God's presence. Her death at Auschwitz testifies that God's goodness can be embraced even when the world appears stripped of it.

St. André Bessette (20th century)

Patron saint of: illness, caregivers, those seeking humility. A humble doorkeeper in Montreal, André had no wealth, education, or status. Yet countless people found healing and hope through his simplicity, gentleness, and unwavering trust in God's goodness. His life reveals that the deepest witness to God's goodness often comes through ordinary, hidden faithfulness rather than grand achievements.

Why Wait?

A year from now, what would it be like to be happier in your work or family or health? I would like to leave you with two things.

First, read the story of *The Giving Tree*. Written by Shel Silverstein, it is only 629 words and illustrated with simple sketches. It begins with a tree who loved the boy who swung from her branches. Each section concludes with the refrain, "And the tree was happy." When the boy became a teenager and needed money, the tree shook apples from its branches for the boy to gather to sell. "And the tree was happy." When the boy grew into a man, the tree gave its branches and then its trunk to him so that he would be happy. The tree in the end had nothing left. But the tree loved the boy. "And the tree was happy...."

Reading the story and looking at the child-like illustrations, I cannot help but get choked up. Something in us is deeply moved by such selfless giving. We want to give ourselves completely like the Giving Tree. At the end of the day, we are happiest when we live to give. Giving out of love, no matter the cost and holding nothing back, we are happiest.

Second, use this way to pray towards happiest. The "Our Father" is the one prayer that Jesus taught. He told us to ask God to act now. For example, "Give us each day our daily bread!" was not a general way to acknowledge the providence of God. For the homeless followers of Jesus who lived hand to mouth, it was the heartfelt difference between going to bed hungry or going to bed with food in the stomach. Each of the seven petitions is similarly urgent. In this light, add the word "today" after each petition:

(1) Our Father, who art in heaven, hallowed be thy name; [today]

(2) thy kingdom come, [today]

(3) thy will be done on earth as it is in heaven. [today]

(4) Give us this day our daily bread, [today]

(5) and forgive us our trespasses, as we forgive those who trespass against us; [today]

(6) and lead us not into temptation, [today]

(7) but deliver us from evil. [today]

Adding the word "today" presses the plea that God act now. Why wait another day? Pray with the urgency of "today" every morning before the day begins rolling. Such a prayer entrusts the new day to the Lord. It surrenders our pursuit of happiness through feeling good, having the goods, and doing good. The prayer helps us to embrace that we are his children and we can depend on him for our happiness. God is good.

Why wait?

Endnotes

1. Maggie Penman, "He Spent Years Asking People If They're Happy. This Is What He Learned," *The Washington Post,* October 10, 2025. www.washingtonpost.com

2. *Are You Happy?* TikTok profile. www.tiktok.com/@areyouhapppy

3. Adam I. Trekwell, "What Is the Prime Directive in Star Trek?," July 19, 2025. www.sciencefictionclassics.com

4. Alexandra Samuel, "The More I Talked to an AI Chatbot, the Less I Talked to Everybody Else," *The Wall Street Journal,* November 2, 2025. www.wsj.com

5. United States Conference of Catholic Bishops, *Create in Me a Pure Heart: Statement on Pornography,* 2025, 1–2. www.usccb.org

6. Covenant Eyes, "PAUS Assessment," accessed November 8, 2025. www.covenanteyes.com

7. Spencer Cox and Ian Marcus Corbin, "America Must Confront Its Crisis of Meaning and Purpose," *The Washington Post,* October 26, 2025. www.washingtonpost.com

8. 2 Kings 5:14; full narrative in 2 Kings 5:1–27.

9. *WhiteBook-Copyright.pdf,* 61. www.sa.org

10. Jared Diamond, "The New York Yankees Just Wasted Another Year of Aaron Judge," *The Wall Street Journal*, October 9, 2025. www.wsj.com

11. Henri J. M. Nouwen, *The Selfless Way of Christ: Downward Mobility and the Spiritual Life* (Maryknoll, NY: Orbis Books, 2013), 25–26.

12. Nouwen, 28.

13. Evan Osnos, *The Haves and the Have-Yachts: Dispatches on the Ultrarich* (New York: Scribner, 2025), 3–4.

14. Pope Leo XIV, Apostolic Exhortation *Dilexi Te*, "On Love for the Poor," October 4, 2025, paragraph 11. www.vatican.va

15. James Bradley, *Flyboys: A True Story of Courage* (Boston: Little, Brown and Company, 2003), 16–28.

16. Tracy Kidder, *A Truck Full of Money* (New York: Random House, 2016), 30–37.

17. Martin Luther King Jr., "On Being a Good Neighbor," draft chapter, March 1, 1963, The Martin Luther King, Jr. Research and Education Institute. https://kinginstitute.stanford.edu

18. John Paul II, Apostolic Letter *Salvifici Doloris*, "On the Christian Meaning of Human Suffering," February 11, 1984. www.vatican.va

19. You do not need to be Christian to stop on your way and help someone. What makes it Christian is why we stop. The Lord saw us beaten by sin, half dead in the ditch. He asked himself, "What will happen to humanity if I do not stop?" It would die and suffer eternal death. He stopped for humankind even though we might hesitate to inconvenience ourselves let alone risk our lives for someone in an opposing social group. Yet Jesus gave his life for us. From his cross, Jesus established his Church and Sacraments through which he heals wounded humanity and restores it to the fullness of life.

20. Howard Primer, "Open and Shut: Scheffler Dominates in British Open Victory for Second Major This Year," *Orlando Sentinel*, July 20, 2025. www.orlandosentinel.com

21. Catholic Truth and Healing, accessed November 8, 2025. https://ctah.archivistsacwr.org/

22. United States Conference of Catholic Bishops, *Indigenous Pastoral Framework*, June 2024. www.usccb.org

23. Pope Francis, Apostolic Journey to Canada: "Meeting with Young People and Elders," Iqaluit, July 29, 2022. www.vatican.va

24. United States Conference of Catholic Bishops, 2024 CYP Annual Report (Digital). www.usccb.org

25. Rudolph J. Rummel, 20th Century Democide, accessed November 8, 2025. www.hawaii.edu/powerkills

26. Father Michael Simone, "The Holiness of the Sabbath," *America Magazine*, September 6, 2025. www.americamagazine.org; see also Anthony Saldarini, "Pharisees," in *The Anchor Bible Dictionary*.